Christ-Centered Christmas

Hal & Melanie Young

GREAT WATERS PRESS
MAKING BIBLICAL FAMILY LIFE PRACTICAL

©2011 Hal & Melanie Young, All Rights Reserved
Great Waters Press

www.GreatWatersPress.com

If purchased in eBook format, this eBook is not licensed for resale. This license is personal to the original purchaser and may not be sold, loaned, or otherwise transferred to third parties or additional users. Purchaser may make one copy for each member of their immediate household. Additional Licenses should be purchased if you'd like to share this eBook with anyone outside your family. Unlimited copies may be made only of pages containing words of Christmas Carols or recipes. Contact info@greatwaterspress.com for information.

Copying for school or co-op use is strictly prohibited. Each student should purchase their own copy.

No part of this publication may otherwise be published, reproduced, stored in a retrieval system, or transmitted or copied in any form or by any means now known or hereafter developed, whether electronic, mechanical, or otherwise, without prior written permission of the publisher. Illegal use, copying, publication, transfer or distribution is considered copyright infringement according to Sections 107 and 108 and other relevant portions of the United States Copyright Act.

The use of any trademarked names does not imply endorsement or approval by the companies holding those trademarks. This document is intended only to enhance your user experience.

Cover art is an original painting by Norma Young, ©2014. Cover Design by John Calvin Young and Melanie Young, ©2016.

Scripture taken from the New King James Version. Copyright © 1982 by Thomas Nelson, Inc. Used by permission. All rights reserved.

Table of Contents

Introduction	5
Decorating	7
Evergreen Garland	9
The Ornament of the Year	11
Granny's Christmas Tea	13
The Advent Season	14
The Christmas Story	15
Prophecy – Believing in the Savior to Come	16
Born that Man No More May Die	18
The Birth of the King	19
Caroling Parties	22
We Three Kings	23
Hark the Herald Angels Sing	24
O Come, O Come Emmanuel	25
Angels From the Realms of Glory	26
O Little Town of Bethlehem	27
God Rest Ye Merry Gentlemen	28
Good Christian Men Rejoice	29
Thou Didst Leave Thy Throne	30
O Come All Ye Faithful	31
Joy to the World	32
It Came Upon a Midnight Clear	33
Silent Night	34
Away in a Manger	35
The First Noel	36
Angels We Have Heard on High	37
O Holy Night	38
Christmas Baking	39
Ingredient Chart	40
Shopping List	41

Christmas Eve	43
Christmas Eve Menu	44
Ham Delights	45
Pigs in Blankets	46
Meat, Cheese & Other Trays	47
Savory Cheese Ball	48
Harral Young's Sugar Cookies	49
Whoopie Pies	50
Cream Wafers	52
Orange Juice Balls	53
Granny's Fruit Cakes	54
Cheese Straws	55
Sausage Balls	55
Other Sweets	56
What About Santa Claus?	61
Christmas Gifts	63
Christmas Day	67
Sausage Muffins	69
Christmas Feast Menu	70
Baked Ham	71
Escalloped Pineapple	72
Browned Rice	73
Seven Layer Salad	74
Nanny's Macaroni and Cheese Pie	75
Sweet Potato Soufflé	76
Chocolate Meringue Pie and Other Pies	77
Old Christmas	79
Other Great Resources	81
Acknowledgements	82

Most of us remember one or two really spectacular Christmas celebrations. It may be the year we received the gift we had really, really hungered for, a treasured toy or tickets for a special event or an article of clothing or a piece of electronic gear. It may be a year marked by something that was only funny after the fact, like the time the cat pulled down the Christmas tree or something set the kitchen curtains on fire. It may be a bittersweet recollection, like the last celebration before the loss of a loved one. It may be a year marked by an unhappy event like the hospitalization of a child, though hopefully these are exceptional.

These are all part of your family history, and in their place they are valid parts of the holiday tradition of your home. However, these are all things which come about because of particular circumstances that year, whether they reflect your current levels of prosperity, the unusual opportunities that arise, or events that simply can't be planned. What about the traditions which are stable, the things which our families look forward to and rejoice to remember in later years?

After all, God ordained holidays in Scripture. They are meant to be times of recollection and teaching, when our families bring back to mind the mercies and wonderful works of God and explain them to our children. In Exodus 12, for example, the Lord gave Moses the ceremonies attached to Passover, and commanded them to be a memorial to the people of Israel. Other days of the year were given for worship and celebration, some solemn and some joyful, but all of them meant to bring families and communities together to reflect on God's purposes and truth.

The New Testament makes it clear that the Jewish holy days are not binding on the followers of Christ. Paul points out that the focus is not on celebration for its own sake, but rather on the Lord. "One person esteems one day above another; another esteems every day alike," he wrote. "Let each be fully convinced in his own mind. He who observes the day, observes it to the Lord; and he who does not observe the day, to the Lord he does not observe it." (Romans 14:5-6). That is really the crux of the matter: it is not whether you celebrate or not, but Who is the center of our celebration!

We decided long ago that celebrating Christmas was not as a matter of biblical obligation – after all, there's no commandment in the Bible to do so – but it is an excellent opportunity to draw the attention of our children, our family, our friends and our acquaintances to the truth of God's Word in a winsome way. We rejoice in the Christmas season like the people around us, but with a difference!

For this reason, we have approached Christmas season with two things in mind. One is to establish our family's traditions that will naturally repeat from year to year and become part of our children's memories even when they are in homes of their own. The Lord helped us with this early in our marriage, as Hal's military assignments took us far away from our parents' homes and forced us to develop our own traditions. It gave us the freedom to really think through what we are doing each year. We have tried to preserve the very best of both of our families' ways as well as adding some new ones to make traditions that we hope will remind our children of the things we've taught them about our Lord.

Second, we've sought out the opportunity to host holiday events for our family and friends. It's a lot of work to clean this house where ten people live (at least during holidays), but it is so worth it to have the freedom to focus our celebrations on Christ and draw the people around us toward Him. Whether our celebrations involve just our children and us or bring a dozen or more of our friends' families together, we rejoice in "the fellowship of kindred minds" in a season that is readymade for open hearts!

Decorating

One of the first signs of the Christmas season is the appearance of decorations.

We understand that some Christians equate traditional decorations with pagan rituals, but there is actually evidence that it was Boniface, a Christian missionary of the 8th century, who introduced the custom of decorating Christian homes with greenery. A bold, manly minister, he confronted the pagan priests of Germany and cut down the Oak of Thor in the center of the sacred grove on Mt. Gudenberg in 723. The priests and villagers were stunned when Thor was unable to avenge himself on Boniface and many were converted. The Oak was used to build a church on the site.

Boniface After Felling the Oak, Carl Emil Doepler, 1905, in *Walhall, die Götterwelt der Germanen*

Shortly thereafter, a boy came to the missionary with a desperate plea to rescue his sister who was due to be sacrificed as the vestal virgin that evening. Boniface rescued her just in time, a wooden cross he carried catching the dagger in its deadly course. Boniface explained to the worshippers that there was no need for a further sacrifice for sin; that Christ had died in our place, the complete and perfect sacrifice, so that we could be forgiven. Boniface then boldly began to hack down the sacred grove. Shaken by the inactivity and incapacity of their idols, the onlookers came to Christ. Boniface gave them the boughs he'd cut and told them to take them home and display them as a tribute to the finished work of Christ. As this occurred during the Advent season which Boniface soon taught them of, decoration with greenery quickly became associated with Christmas in Germany.

Much later, Martin Luther, the Reformer, introduced the use of lights, originally candles, on Christmas trees because they reminded him of God's stars he saw through the branches of trees in the forest.

In our home, evergreens remind us of the gift of eternal life. Red ribbons represent Christ's blood; white symbolizes His purity; gold recalls His majesty. Wreaths are circles because circles have no beginning and no end, just as God has no beginning and no end and everlasting life does not end. We use lights because Jesus is the light of the world and we are to be lights in the midst of a dark and perverse generation, among whom we shine as lights in the world. Angels remind us of the angels that heralded Christ's birth and stars recall the star that guided the wise men to Him. Holly reminds us of the crown of thorns and the berries of the drops of His blood. Fruit is the fruit of the Spirit. Bells remind of us church bells calling us to worship.

We love to make our own wreaths and garland. It's really quite easy. We just collect evergreen boughs from the woods or ask a Christmas tree seller if we can have the branches he's trimmed off the bottom of trees. Here's how to make a garland:

Evergreen Garland

Evergreen boughs
Small pruning shears (in a pinch, wire cutters or even your dog's nail clippers will work)
22 or 24 gauge wire
(Optional) Lemons, limes, or other fruit; ribbons; other Christmas decorations

Cut the boughs into sprigs about 10 to 12 inches long. Pick up a few sprigs of evergreen and wind them together with wire. Don't cut the wire! Add another handful of sprigs to the stem of the first, with the tops pointing the same way but slid down further, wiring them to the first group by just wrapping the paddle of wire around both of them a few times. Pick up another handful and do the same thing. Continue until the garland is long enough for your purpose. Turn the last sprig the opposite direction and wire it to the next to last bunch. We put a large nail at each corner of our front porch and drape the garland across it.

Once you've made a garland, you can make a wreath very easily the same way. Find a sturdy, but flexible longer branch and bend it into a circle shape. If you don't have one long enough, wire two or more, or a whole handful of thinner branches together. Choose a starting point and wrap the paddle around the wreath form branches and around a handful of sprigs. Move over a bit and pick up another handful of sprigs. Use the top of the sprigs to cover the wire you just wrapped (Point the sprigs all the same way!) and wire them to the wreath the same way.

Continue all around the wreath, making it as full as you desire. When you get back to where you started, lift the top of that very first sprig, stick the stems of the last sprig under it and wire them down. These wreaths smell wonderful!!

I like to decorate it Williamsburg style: wiring lemons and limes or apples to the wreath. Just get a straight piece of wire and holding it close to the point, aim it right at the side of the fruit. Just jab it in and smoothly push it through the fruit - it will pop out on the other side. Pull the wire halfway through, then use the two ends to wire the fruit to the wreath.

I like to add a big red bow, too. Christmas tree decorations (glass balls in particular) are lovely wired into the garland, as well. You can make small garlands to decorate your tables and mantles, too. Just lay the garland down the center of the table, using a curving, winding path. It's lovely to wind gold beads around it, or ribbon, or to decorate with fruit or pinecones.

The Ornament of the Year

Christmas had always been a special time in both our families growing up. Our mothers made many of the ornaments on our tree, we had certain foods that were always served, there were certain activities the family always did. Our first Christmas together after our marriage found us over a thousand miles away from our childhood homes and we felt a little bleak as we considered how to celebrate. Just about the time we decided to go buy a live Christmas tree, a couple of unexpected boxes showed up on our doorstep. One of the boxes, from Hal's grandmother, had a handmade tree skirt, lights, a "First Christmas Together" ornament, and a collection of crocheted ornaments she had made for our tree: snowflakes, stockings, snowmen and more. I have never heard of a more thoughtful Christmas gift for a new couple. Our tree immediately became warm and homey!

The next box, from Hal's mother, contained ornaments that had been Hal's growing up – the ornaments he saw on his childhood tree year after year. Melanie was so grateful to share that piece of his childhood with him.

Those two wonderful ladies inspired us as we looked at the tree which had a few hours earlier been so impersonal and cold. We wanted to always have a tree that was full of memories! We decided right then, long before we had children, that each year we would choose an ornament that would remind us of God's doings in our family that year. We would buy one for ourselves and one for each of our children. When they married and left home, we would send them a box of each year's "ornament of the year," a box of memories to share with their mates. We've done that now for over twenty-five years.

The day we decorate the tree is greatly anticipated in our home. We serve party foods instead of dinner; things like meatballs and cheese ball with crackers, chips and dip, and eggnog. Eggnog is a favorite in our house (non-alcoholic and generally diluted with milk) and the day we decorate the tree is the first time we drink eggnog in the season. The look of awe in the baby's eyes when they first see a tree in the house – "What in the world?" – is delightful!

We take time to remind our children that the use of a Christmas tree is not described in Scripture, but it is one way we can show our joy in God's gift of Jesus Christ to us and remind ourselves of what He has done for us. The fresh evergreen reminds us of eternal life, that there is coming a time when death shall be no more. The lights remind us that Jesus is the light of the world.

Each year as we decorate the tree, we tell the stories behind each ornament. When we unpack the blown glass cornucopias, we tell our children about the year that Hal had been laid off and God's provided abundantly for our family's needs. The little models of Wright Brothers' plane remind us of the year our family made a movie about Orville and Wilber, and the director's clapboards commemorate the year our boys' films did extremely well in competition. The tiny life jackets remind us of the year we discovered self-employment meant Hal could work anywhere, even for weeks at a time by the lake! The hearts memorialize the year our Katie's heart was healed. The ornaments that others have given enable us to talk about them and their roles in our lives as well. As we unpack each ornament and place it on the tree, God's incredible blessings to our family, in hard times and in good, become obvious to all of us. Decades of memories hang on our tree.

Granny's Christmas Tea

Norma Young

2 quarts weak tea (herbal orange or apple will work instead of tea.)
2 cups sugar
6 Tablespoons lemon juice (or juice of 3 lemons)
1 ½ - 4 cups orange juice (or juice of 3+ oranges to taste)
1 quart pineapple juice (or up to a whole can to taste)
2 Tablespoons whole cloves, steeped in…1 cup boiling water

Steep cloves for at least 15-30 minutes in boiling water, strain out cloves and add clove-water to the rest of ingredients. Combine and warm until hot tea temperature. A wonderful holiday treat that everyone loves – children, too. We make it by the stockpot full and keep in the refrigerator all season.

Makes about one gallon.

This exquisite tea is a hallmark of the holiday season at our house.

The Advent Season

Anticipation builds excitement and makes an event memorable. We've done a variety of things over the years to build anticipation in the advent season with our children.

One of our favorites is to continue our Hymn of the Week tradition, in which we learn a new hymn each week, but to use Christmas carols during this time. Using a different one each week, we sing the entire song every day, and each day explain one of the verses. This builds up a store of hymns that they know by heart – and gives them a way to worship as they go along through life.

We've also used some of the advent books available. Jotham's Journey and its sequels by Arnold Ytreeide are adventurous historical fiction set in the time of Christ. The stories are broken up into daily readings through the Advent season. Our guys really enjoyed them, though they are sometimes a little fantastic.

Last year we used Amy Puetz's Countdown to Christmas and really enjoyed it. It contains classic and forgotten stories and activities for each day in December leading up to Christmas.

Several of our friends use an Advent wreath. An Advent is a horizontal, table-top wreath with four usually red candles for each week in Advent, and often one white candle, the Christ candle, in the center. Some light them once a week,

others every evening during family worship, lighting a new candle each week until all are lit, including the Christ candle, on Christmas Eve.

Regardless of how you build anticipation for Christmas, we encourage you to do something to focus on the meaning – the story of what God has done.

The Christmas Story

The Adoration of the Magi, Albrecht Durer

Commissioned by Frederick the Wise, who would become the Patron of Martin Luther

Prophecy – Believing in the Savior to Come

...And I will put enmity
Between you and the woman,
And between your seed and her Seed;
He shall bruise your head,
And you shall bruise His heel."

Genesis 3:15

Therefore the Lord Himself will give you a sign: Behold, the virgin shall conceive and bear a Son, and shall call His name Immanuel.

Isaiah 7:14

The Virgin in Prayer, Sassoferrato, 17th century

For unto us a Child is born,
Unto us a Son is given;
And the government will be upon His shoulder.
And His name will be called
Wonderful, Counselor, Mighty God,
Everlasting Father, Prince of Peace.
Of the increase of His government and peace
There will be no end,

Isaiah 9:6-7

"But you, Bethlehem Ephrathah,
    Though you are little among the thousands of Judah,
    Yet out of you shall come forth to Me
    The One to be Ruler in Israel,
    Whose goings forth are from of old,
    From everlasting."

                                                    Micah 5:2

"For dogs have surrounded Me;
    The congregation of the wicked has enclosed Me.
    They pierced[c] My hands and My feet;
I can count all My bones.
    They look and stare at Me.
They divide My garments among them,
    And for My clothing they cast lots."

                                                 Psalm 22: 16-18

Anna and Simeon Recognize the Babe as the Promised Messiah, Rembrandt

Born That Man No More May Die

Who has believed our report?
  And to whom has the arm of the LORD been revealed?
  For He shall grow up before Him as a tender plant,
    And as a root out of dry ground.

He has no form or comeliness;
  And when we see Him,
  There is no beauty that we should desire Him.
  He is despised and rejected by men,
    A Man of sorrows and acquainted with grief.

And we hid, as it were, our faces from Him;
He was despised, and we did not esteem Him.
Surely He has borne our griefs
And carried our sorrows;
Yet we esteemed Him stricken,
Smitten by God, and afflicted.
But He was wounded for our transgressions,
He was bruised for our iniquities;
The chastisement for our peace was upon Him,
And by His stripes we are healed.
All we like sheep have gone astray;
We have turned, every one, to his own way;
And the LORD has laid on Him the iniquity of us all.

He was oppressed and He was afflicted,
Yet He opened not His mouth;
He was led as a lamb to the slaughter,
And as a sheep before its shearers is silent,
So He opened not His mouth.
He was taken from prison and from judgment,
And who will declare His generation?
For He was cut off from the land of the living;
For the transgressions of My people He was stricken.

And they made His grave with the wicked—
But with the rich at His death,
Because He had done no violence,
Nor was any deceit in His mouth.
Yet it pleased the LORD to bruise Him;
He has put Him to grief.
When You make His soul an offering for sin,
He shall see His seed, He shall prolong His days,
And the pleasure of the LORD shall prosper in His hand.
He shall see the labor of His soul, and be satisfied.
By His knowledge My righteous Servant shall justify many,
For He shall bear their iniquities.
Therefore I will divide Him a portion with the great,
And He shall divide the spoil with the strong,
Because He poured out His soul unto death,
And He was numbered with the transgressors,
And He bore the sin of many,
And made intercession for the transgressors.

Isaiah 53

The Birth of the King

And it came to pass in those days that a decree went out from Caesar Augustus that all the world should be registered. This census first took place while Quirinius was governing Syria. So all went to be registered, everyone to his own city. Joseph also went up from Galilee, out of the city of Nazareth, into Judea, to the city of David, which is called Bethlehem, because he was of the house and lineage of David, to be registered with Mary, his betrothed wife, who was with child. So it was, that while they were there, the days were completed for her to be delivered. And she brought forth her firstborn Son, and wrapped Him in swaddling cloths, and laid Him in a manger, because there was no room for them in the inn.

Now there were in the same country shepherds living out in the fields, keeping watch over their flock by night. And behold, an angel of the Lord stood before them, and the glory of the Lord shone around them, and they were greatly afraid. Then the angel said to them, "Do not be afraid, for behold, I bring you good tidings of great joy which will be to all people. For there is born to you this day in the city of David a Savior, who is Christ the Lord. And this will be the sign to you: You will find a Babe wrapped in swaddling cloths, lying in a manger." And suddenly there was with the angel a multitude of the heavenly host praising God and saying:

" Glory to God in the highest,
And on earth peace, goodwill toward men!"

Annunciation to the Shepherds, Benjamin-Gerritsz Cuyp

So it was, when the angels had gone away from them into heaven, that the shepherds said to one another, "Let us now go to Bethlehem and see this thing that has come to pass, which the Lord has made known to us." And they came with haste and found Mary and Joseph, and the Babe lying in a manger. Now when they had seen Him, they made widely known the saying which was told them concerning this Child. And all those who heard it marveled at those things which were told them by the shepherds. But Mary kept all these things and pondered them in her heart. Then the shepherds returned, glorifying and praising God for all the things that they had heard and seen, as it was told them.

Luke 2:1-20

Adoration of the Shepherds, Rembrandt

Caroling Parties

Christmas is the only time of year that it is not only socially acceptable, but considered a gift to knock on stranger's doors and sing hymns full of gospel truth to them! We don't want this tradition to ever die out, so every year we invite like-minded families to come caroling with us.

We invite families to come just after supper and we meet in our front yard so folks don't have to remove their wraps. We try to have hymnals or the words to the carols we plan to sing copied for everyone. We walk around the neighborhood, knocking wherever we see lights. When people come to the door, we just begin singing. We do sing more than one verse of the carols because it's often the middle verses that contain the most truth! We keep it to one or two carols per house, though, unless they seem really excited about us singing more. We end with "We Wish You a Merry Christmas" and shout, "Merry Christmas!" and leave.

What a blessing to be able to share the words of life with our neighbors so easily! When our voices give out, we return to our house for refreshments. We usually put on a spread like we do for Christmas Eve, but perhaps a little lighter, since folks have already had supper. This is one of our favorite times of the season!

Our local homeschool history club goes caroling downtown every year in historical costumes. Our whole town looks forward to it and talks about it. The past several years, they've been asked to do it on the eve of the town's Christmas tree lighting and to come early and sing at the town's ceremony and to perform at the Festival of Trees. What a delight to fill the air with praises to our Savior and in the form of songs that people associate with joy and happiness.

Take a look at those old Christmas hymns and read the words of those middle verses. What a privilege to share that with the world!

WE THREE KINGS

If you only sing the first verse and refrain you miss the awesome message that Christ came to die for us! It was written by John H. Hopkins, Jr. for a Christmas pageant at General Theological Seminary in New York City in 1857.

We three kings of Orient are;
Bearing gifts we traverse afar,
Field and fountain, moor and mountain,
Following yonder star.

*O star of wonder, star of light,
Star with royal beauty bright,
Westward leading, still proceeding,
Guide us to thy perfect light.*

Born a King on Bethlehem's plain
Gold I bring to crown Him again,
King forever, ceasing never,
Over us all to reign.

*O star of wonder, star of light,
Star with royal beauty bright,
Westward leading, still proceeding,
Guide us to thy perfect light.*

Frankincense to offer have I;
Incense owns a Deity nigh;
Prayer and praising, voices raising,
Worshipping God on high.

*O star of wonder, star of light,
Star with royal beauty bright,
Westward leading, still proceeding,
Guide us to thy perfect light.*

Myrrh is mine, its bitter perfume
Breathes a life of gathering gloom;
Sorrowing, sighing, bleeding, dying,
Sealed in the stone cold tomb.

*O star of wonder, star of light,
Star with royal beauty bright,
Westward leading, still proceeding,
Guide us to thy perfect light.*

Glorious now behold Him arise;
King and God and sacrifice;
Alleluia, Alleluia,
Sounds through the earth and skies.

*O star of wonder, star of light,
Star with royal beauty bright,
Westward leading, still proceeding,
Guide us to thy perfect light.*

Hark the Herald Angels Sing!

This lovely hymn by Charles Wesley is more full of truth than many sermons and can imprint these precious truths on our hearts.
Felix Mendelssohn composed the melody in his cantata celebrating the 400th anniversary of Gutenberg's invention of the printing press.

Hark! The herald angels sing,
"Glory to the newborn King;
Peace on earth, and mercy mild,
God and sinners reconciled!"
Joyful, all ye nations rise,
Join the triumph of the skies;
With th'angelic host proclaim,
"Christ is born in Bethlehem!"

Refrain
Hark! the herald angels sing,
"Glory to the newborn King!"

Christ, by highest Heav'n adored;
Christ the everlasting Lord;
Late in time, behold Him come,
Offspring of a virgin's womb.
Veiled in flesh the Godhead see;
Hail th'incarnate Deity,
Pleased with us in flesh to dwell,
Jesus our Emmanuel.

Refrain

Hail the heav'nly Prince of Peace!
Hail the Sun of Righteousness!
Light and life to all He brings,
Ris'n with healing in His wings.
Mild He lays His glory by,
Born that man no more may die.
Born to raise the sons of earth,
Born to give them second birth.

Refrain

Come, Desire of nations, come,
Fix in us Thy humble home;
Rise, the woman's conqu'ring Seed,
Bruise in us the serpent's head.
Adam's likeness, Lord, efface,
Stamp Thine image in its place:
Second Adam from above,
Reinstate us in Thy love.

Refrain

O Come, O Come, Emmanuel

Every verse of this song comes from the precious prophecies of the Messiah. The words are some 700 years old, the music 500 years old. We like to sing at least the last refrain, "Emmanuel has come to thee, O Israel."

O come, O come, Emmanuel,
And ransom captive Israel,
That mourns in lonely exile here
Until the Son of God appear.

Rejoice! Rejoice!
Emmanuel shall come to thee, O Israel.

O come, Thou Wisdom from on high,
Who orderest all things mightily;
To us the path of knowledge show,
And teach us in her ways to go.

Rejoice! Rejoice!
Emmanuel shall come to thee, O Israel.

O come, Thou Rod of Jesse, free
Thine own from Satan's tyranny;
From depths of hell Thy people save,
And give them victory over the grave.

Rejoice! Rejoice!
Emmanuel shall come to thee, O Israel.

O come, Thou Day-spring, come and cheer
Our spirits by Thine advent here;
Disperse the gloomy clouds of night,
And death's dark shadows put to flight.

Rejoice! Rejoice!
Emmanuel shall come to thee, O Israel.

O come, Thou Key of David, come,
And open wide our heavenly home;
Make safe the way that leads on high,
And close the path to misery.

Rejoice! Rejoice!
Emmanuel shall come to thee, O Israel.

O come, O come, great Lord of might,
Who to Thy tribes on Sinai's height
In ancient times once gave the law
In cloud and majesty and awe.

Rejoice! Rejoice!
Emmanuel shall come to thee, O Israel.

O come, Thou Root of Jesse's tree,
An ensign of Thy people be;
Before Thee rulers silent fall;
All peoples on Thy mercy call.

Rejoice! Rejoice!
Emmanuel shall come to thee, O Israel.

O come, Desire of nations, bind
In one the hearts of all mankind;
Bid Thou our sad divisions cease,
And be Thyself our King of Peace.

Rejoice! Rejoice!
Emmanuel shall come to thee, O Israel.

Angels from the Realms of Glory

The whole Christmas story in a song!

Angels from the realms of glory,
Wing your flight o'er all the earth;
Ye who sang creation's story
Now proclaim Messiah's birth.

Refrain

*Come and worship, come and worship,
Worship Christ, the newborn King.*

Shepherds, in the field abiding,
Watching o'er your flocks by night,
God with us is now residing;
Yonder shines the infant light:

Refrain

Sages, leave your contemplations,
Brighter visions beam afar;
Seek the great Desire of nations;
Ye have seen His natal star.

Refrain

Saints, before the altar bending,
Watching long in hope and fear;
Suddenly the Lord, descending,
In His temple shall appear.

Refrain

Sinners, wrung with true repentance,
Doomed for guilt to endless pains,
Justice now revokes the sentence,
Mercy calls you; break your chains.

Refrain

Though an Infant now we view Him,
He shall fill His Father's throne,
Gather all the nations to Him;
Every knee shall then bow down:

Refrain

All creation, join in praising
God, the Father, Spirit, Son,
Evermore your voices raising
To th'eternal Three in One.

Refrain

O Little Town of Bethlehem

O little town of Bethlehem, how still we see thee lie!
Above thy deep and dreamless sleep the silent stars go by.
Yet in thy dark streets shineth the everlasting Light;
The hopes and fears of all the years are met in thee tonight.

For Christ is born of Mary, and gathered all above,
While mortals sleep, the angels keep their watch of wondering love.
O morning stars together, proclaim the holy birth,
And praises sing to God the King, and peace to men on earth!

How silently, how silently, the wondrous Gift is giv'n;
So God imparts to human hearts the blessings of His Heav'n.
No ear may hear His coming, but in this world of sin,
Where meek souls will receive Him still, the dear Christ enters in.

O holy Child of Bethlehem, descend to us, we pray;
Cast out our sin, and enter in, be born in us today.
We hear the Christmas angels the great glad tidings tell;
O come to us, abide with us, our Lord Emmanuel!

God Rest Ye Merry Gentlemen

God rest ye merry, gentlemen, let nothing you dismay,
Remember Christ our Savior was born on Christmas Day;
To save us all from Satan's power when we were gone astray.

O tidings of comfort and joy, comfort and joy; O tidings of comfort and joy.

In Bethlehem, in Israel, this blessèd Babe was born,
And laid within a manger upon this blessèd morn;
The which His mother Mary did nothing take in scorn.

Refrain

From God our heavenly Father a blessèd angel came;
And unto certain shepherds brought tidings of the same;
How that in Bethlehem was born the Son of God by name.

Refrain

"Fear not, then," said the angel, "Let nothing you afright
This day is born a Savior of a pure Virgin bright,
To free all those who trust in Him from Satan's power and might."

Refrain

The shepherds at those tidings rejoiced much in mind,
And left their flocks a-feeding in tempest, storm and wind,
And went to Bethl'em straightaway this blessèd Babe to find.

Refrain

But when to Bethlehem they came where our dear Savior lay,
They found Him in a manger where oxen feed on hay;
His mother Mary kneeling unto the Lord did pray.

Refrain

Now to the Lord sing praises all you within this place,
And with true love and brotherhood each other now embrace;
This holy tide of Christmas all others doth deface.

Refrain

God bless the ruler of this house, and send him long to reign,
And many a merry Christmas may live to see again;
Among your friends and kindred that live both far and near—

That God send you a happy new year, happy new year, And God send you a happy new year.

Good Christian Men Rejoice

The words and music of this carol date back to the 1300s!

Good Christian men, rejoice with heart and soul, and voice;
Give ye heed to what we say: Jesus Christ is born today;
Ox and ass before Him bow; and He is in the manger now.
Christ is born today! Christ is born today!

Good Christian men, rejoice, with heart and soul and voice;
Now ye hear of endless bliss: Jesus Christ was born for this!
He has opened the heavenly door, and man is blest forevermore.
Christ was born for this! Christ was born for this!

Good Christian men, rejoice, with heart and soul and voice;
Now ye need not fear the grave: Jesus Christ was born to save!
Calls you one and calls you all, to gain His everlasting hall.
Christ was born to save! Christ was born to save!

Thou Didst Leave Thy Throne

This carol helps us to understand just what the Lord did for us.

Thou didst leave Thy throne and Thy kingly crown,
When Thou camest to earth for me;
But in Bethlehem's home was there found no room
For Thy holy nativity.

Refrain

O come to my heart, Lord Jesus,
There is room in my heart for Thee.

Heaven's arches rang when the angels sang,
Proclaiming Thy royal degree;
But of lowly birth didst Thou come to earth,
And in great humility.

Refrain

The foxes found rest, and the birds their nest
In the shade of the forest tree;
But Thy couch was the sod, O Thou Son of God,
In the deserts of Galilee.

Refrain

Thou camest, O Lord, with the living Word,
That should set Thy people free;
But with mocking scorn and with crown of thorn,
They bore Thee to Calvary.

Refrain

When the heav'ns shall ring, and her choirs shall sing,
At Thy coming to victory,
Let Thy voice call me home, saying "Yet there is room,
There is room at My side for thee."

My heart shall rejoice, Lord Jesus,
When Thou comest and callest for me

O Come All Ye Faithful

The words of the second verse are directly from one of the oldest creeds.

O come, all ye faithful, joyful and triumphant,
O come ye, O come ye, to Bethlehem.
Come and behold Him, born the King of angels;

Refrain

O come, let us adore Him,
O come, let us adore Him,
O come, let us adore Him,
Christ the Lord.

God of God, Light of Lights,
Lo, He abhors not the Virgin's womb;
Son of the Father, begotten, not created;

Refrain

Sing, choirs of angels, sing in exultation;
O sing, all ye citizens of heaven above!
Glory to God, all glory in the highest;

Refrain

Yea, Lord, we greet Thee, born this happy morning;
Jesus, to Thee be glory given;
Word of the Father, now in flesh appearing.

Refrain

Joy to the World

Written by Isaac Watts, this old favorite well expresses the joy of Christmas.

Joy to the world, the Lord is come!
Let earth receive her King;
Let every heart prepare Him room,
And Heaven and nature sing,
And Heaven and nature sing,
And Heaven, and Heaven, and nature sing.

Joy to the earth, the Savior reigns!
Let men their songs employ;
While fields and floods, rocks, hills and plains
Repeat the sounding joy,
Repeat the sounding joy,
Repeat, repeat, the sounding joy.

No more let sins and sorrows grow,
Nor thorns infest the ground;
He comes to make His blessings flow
Far as the curse is found,
Far as the curse is found,
Far as, far as, the curse is found.

He rules the world with truth and grace,
And makes the nations prove
The glories of His righteousness,
And wonders of His love,
And wonders of His love,
And wonders, wonders, of His love.

It Came Upon the Midnight Clear

It came upon the midnight clear,
That glorious song of old,
From angels bending near the earth,
To touch their harps of gold;
"Peace on the earth, good will to men,
From Heaven's all gracious King."
The world in solemn stillness lay,
To hear the angels sing.

Still through the cloven skies they come
With peaceful wings unfurled,
And still their heavenly music floats
O'er all the weary world;
Above its sad and lowly plains,
They bend on hovering wing,
And ever over its Babel sounds
The blessèd angels sing.

Yet with the woes of sin and strife
The world has suffered long;
Beneath the angel strain have rolled
Two thousand years of wrong;
And man, at war with man, hears not
The love-song which they bring;
O hush the noise, ye men of strife
And hear the angels sing.

And ye, beneath life's crushing load,
Whose forms are bending low,
Who toil along the climbing way
With painful steps and slow,
Look now! for glad and golden hours
Come swiftly on the wing.
O rest beside the weary road,
And hear the angels sing!

For lo! the days are hastening on,
By prophet-bards foretold,
When with the ever circling years
Comes round the age of gold;
When peace shall over all the earth
Its ancient splendors fling,
And the whole world send back the song
Which now the angels sing.

Silent Night

Silent night, holy night,
All is calm, all is bright
Round yon virgin mother and Child.
Holy Infant, so tender and mild,
Sleep in heavenly peace,
Sleep in heavenly peace.

Silent night, holy night,
Shepherds quake at the sight;
Glories stream from heaven afar,
Heavenly hosts sing Alleluia!
Christ the Savior is born,
Christ the Savior is born!

Silent night, holy night,
Son of God, love's pure light;
Radiant beams from Thy holy face
With the dawn of redeeming grace,
Jesus, Lord, at Thy birth,
Jesus, Lord, at Thy birth.

Silent night, holy night
Wondrous star, lend thy light;
With the angels let us sing,
Alleluia to our King;
Christ the Savior is born,
Christ the Savior is born!

Away in a Manger

Called Luther's Cradle Hymn

Away in a manger, no crib for a bed,
The little Lord Jesus laid down His sweet head.
The stars in the sky looked down where He lay,
The little Lord Jesus, asleep on the hay.

The cattle are lowing, the Baby awakes,
But little Lord Jesus, no crying He makes;
I love Thee, Lord Jesus, look down from the sky
And stay by my cradle till morning is nigh.

Be near me, Lord Jesus, I ask Thee to stay
Close by me forever, and love me, I pray;
Bless all the dear children in Thy tender care,
And fit us for Heaven to live with Thee there.

THE FIRST NOEL

Dates back to the 13th century!

The first Noel the angel did say
Was to certain poor shepherds in fields as they lay;
In fields where they lay tending their sheep,
On a cold winter's night that was so deep.

Refrain

Noel, Noel, Noel, Noel,
Born is the King of Israel.

They lookèd up and saw a star
Shining in the east, beyond them far;
And to the earth it gave great light,
And so it continued both day and night.

Refrain

And by the light of that same star
Three Wise Men came from country far;
To seek for a King was their intent,
And to follow the star wherever it went.

Refrain

This star drew nigh to the northwest,
Over Bethlehem it took its rest;
And there it did both stop and stay,
Right over the place where Jesus lay.

Refrain

Then did they know assuredly
Within that house the King did lie;
One entered it them for to see,
And found the Babe in poverty.

Refrain

Then entered in those Wise Men three,
Full reverently upon the knee,
And offered there, in His presence,
Their gold and myrrh and frankincense.

Refrain

Between an ox stall and an ass,
This Child truly there He was;
For want of clothing they did Him lay
All in a manger, among the hay.

Refrain

Then let us all with one accord
Sing praises to our heavenly Lord;
That hath made Heaven and earth of naught,
And with His blood mankind hath bought.

Refrain

Angels We Have Heard on High

A traditional French carol.

Angels we have heard on high
Sweetly singing o'er the plains,
And the mountains in reply
Echoing their joyous strains.

Refrain

Gloria, in excelsis Deo!
Gloria, in excelsis Deo!

Shepherds, why this jubilee?
Why your joyous strains prolong?
What the gladsome tidings be
Which inspire your heavenly song?

Refrain

Come to Bethlehem and see
Christ Whose birth the angels sing;
Come, adore on bended knee,
Christ the Lord, the newborn King.

Refrain

See Him in a manger laid,
Whom the choirs of angels praise;
Mary, Joseph, lend your aid,
While our hearts in love we raise.

Refrain

O Holy Night

Difficult to sing, but a favorite of many. Said to be the first music broadcast over the radio.

O holy night, the stars are brightly shining;
It is the night of the dear Savior's birth!
Long lay the world in sin and error pining,
Till He appeared and the soul felt its worth.
A thrill of hope, the weary soul rejoices,
For yonder breaks a new and glorious morn.
Fall on your knees, O hear the angel voices!
O night divine, O night when Christ was born!
O night, O holy night, O night divine!

Led by the light of faith serenely beaming,
With glowing hearts by His cradle we stand.
So led by light of a star sweetly gleaming,
Here came the wise men from Orient land.
The King of kings lay thus in lowly manger,
In all our trials born to be our Friend!
He knows our need—to our weakness is no stranger.
Behold your King; before Him lowly bend!
Behold your King; before Him lowly bend!

Truly He taught us to love one another;
His law is love and His Gospel is peace.
Chains shall He break for the slave is our brother
And in His Name all oppression shall cease.
Sweet hymns of joy in grateful chorus raise we,
Let all within us praise His holy Name!
Christ is the Lord! O praise His name forever!
His pow'r and glory evermore proclaim!
His pow'r and glory evermore proclaim!

Christmas Baking

Hal's father was an extraordinary baker in his free time. We inherited some of the most wonderful recipes from him and from Melanie's family that it's no wonder that we bake like crazy at Christmas. We have about 10 or 12 different kinds of cookies and baked goods we bake every single year. There would probably be a riot if we left something out.

The Lord has graciously provided even for that. One year, friends of ours in Christian ministry were really struggling. Donations were down and there was just no money to pay salary. The children were so excited when we went to the grocery store to pick out baking supplies to take them. We know from experience that you'll do what it takes to provide basic, nourishing food for your family, but in times like those, you let everything extra, all the treats and desserts, go by the wayside. It was so much fun to see their faces when we brought them everything they would need for their Christmas baking. That family became close friends of ours and grew to know our family well and understand how much baking meant to us. Imagine our surprise and delight many years later when we were struggling and they showed up at our house, providing for our Christmas baking! God is so good! It is such a blessing to see His love and provision through the love of the brethren.

I am a firm believer in planning in advance. I make a chart, like a spreadsheet, and list everything I'm making down one side and the common ingredients across the top. I put all the ingredients needed in that chart, so I can shop all at once for our Christmas baking instead of continually running to the store to pick up some more butter or get some more sugar.

I also make a schedule for baking. For example, some cookies require making the dough in advance and chilling over night. Why not make several of these recipes the day I bake fruitcakes and tie up the oven for 3 hours?

And no, some fruitcake is exquisite! Ours is! It's Hal's grandmother's recipe and it converted me.

I always make sausage balls on the same day as cheese straws. They have a lot of the same ingredients and can bake in the oven at the same time at the same temperature and have compatible odors. Makes cleanup and cooking easier – older children can make the sausage balls, and the ones too young to be trusted around the raw pork, can make the cheese straws. And I have *finally* learned not to worry about the children not making the cookies as perfectly as I would – it's going to be eaten anyway!

By just doing a couple of recipes that fit together well a day, I can fill a banquet table with homecooked goodness without stressing myself out. And motivate the children, too – we'll bake cookies as soon as the schoolwork is done!

Christmas Baking Spreadsheet

Recipe	Whoopie Pies	Sausage Balls	Cranberry Braid	Orange Juice Balls	Granny's Fruit Cake	Cream Wafers	Cheese Straws	Cordial Cookies	Papa Young's Sugar Cookies
Batches?	x1	x2	x1	x2	x1	x3	x2	x2	x2
Flour	4 1/4 c flour	5c flour	6c flour		4c flour	6c flour	4c flour	3c flour	6 1/2c flour
Sugars	1 1/4 cup sugar		1 2/3c sugar	2lb confectioner's sugar	1lb brown sugar	2 1/4c conf sugar (about 2/3lb)		2c sugar	3c sugar
Eggs	2 eggs		4 eggs		6 eggs			2 eggs	4 eggs
Butter, Oil	1/2 cup butter +3T (3/8 lb)	3/8 lb butter	3/4c butter (3/8 lb)	1/2 lb butter	1lb butter	3 3/4c butter (2 pound)	1lb butter	1c butter (1/2 lb)	1 1/3c butter (3/4 lb)
Leavening/Seasoning	1t baking soda, 1 1/2 t salt, 1/2 t	1 1/2t salt, 3T baking powder	1 T cornstarch		1t baking powder		1/2t red pepper, 1 1/2t salt	1/2t soda, 1/2t salt	5t baking powder, 1t salt
Liquid Flavorings	1 t vanilla		1/3c orange juice	12 oz orange juice concentrat	1 1/2oz lemon extract	1T vanilla		1t vanilla	4t vanilla, 1 t almond extract
Other Ingredients	2 cup milk, 3/4 cup cocoa, 3/4 cup shortening	1lb sharp cheese, 1lb hot, 1lb mild sausage, Worcestershire	orange rind, 12 oz cranberries, 4 1/2 t yeast	2lb vanilla wafers, coconut	1lb candied cherries, 1/2 lb candied pineapple	1 cup cream, food coloring	1lb sharp cheese, 4 c Rice Krispies	1 cup cocoa, 96 maraschino cherries, 1 c sweetened condensed milk, 12 oz chocolate chips	4T milk

Shopping List for Christmas Baking

10 lb all-purpose flour (38 ¾ cups flour, 1lb=4cups, so I need almost 10lb)

4 or 5lb sugar (a little over 8 cups sugar, 1lb=2cups, so I need a little over 4 lb)

3lb confectioner's sugar

1lb brown sugar, light

18 eggs

7 lb butter (I need 6 7/8 lb)

Sharp cheese, 2lb

Sausage, 1lb hot, 1lb mild

2 ¼ cups milk

1 cup cream

Orange Juice Concentrate, 12oz

Baking Powder (I'll need 16 teaspoonfuls), Baking Soda (1 ½ t), Salt (6 t)

Cayenne or red pepper, ½ t

Vanilla extract, 9t

Almond extract, 1t

Lemon extract, **1 ½ oz**

Yeast, 4 ½ t or 2 packages

Shortening, ¾ cup

Cocoa, 1 ¾ cups

Maraschino Cherries, 96 (2-3 bottles, depending on size of cherries)

Chocolate Chips, 12 oz

Sweetened Condensed Milk, 1 cup

Rice Krispies, 4 cups

Candied Fruit, ½ pound each: green cherries, red cherries, pineapple

Vanilla wafers, 2lb

Orange, 1 (for rind and 1/3 cup orange juice)

Cranberries, 12oz

Food Coloring

Christmas Eve

One of the best days of the year for our family is Christmas Eve. We have a glorious party. The house is decorated. The dining room table is covered with the fanciest dishes we own – silver and china are full of party foods, canapés, hors d'oeuvres, and sweets. Who are the guests for such a spread? Sometimes it is our friends or extended family, but we do the same thing even if it is just our immediate family! We want our children to know that they are precious gifts of God and are worth the best we have to offer – just like "company."

Practically, we believe it is a very good thing for children to know how to behave themselves at a formal party. They will find themselves at gatherings like that throughout their lives. When should they learn how to manage themselves in a buffet line, or how to eat standing or sitting without a table? Why not at home?

During the evening, we pray for the Lord's blessing, then we serve buffet style and eat in the living room – a real rarity at our house. During the evening, Hal reads the Christmas story aloud, we sing carols, visit, talk, and eat. I try not to notice how much the children are eating – or what – this night!

We love our Christmas Eve party whether it is just us or a huge crowd and we've done it both ways.

Christmas Eve Menu

Savory
Ham Delights
Pigs in Blankets
Sausage Balls
Deli Meat Tray
Variety Cheese Tray
Mustard & Mayonnaise
Variety Breads
Savory Cheese Ball
Pepper Jelly on Cream Cheese
Veggie Bars or Vegetable Tray

Crunchy
Potato and Tortilla chips
French Onion Dip
Salsa
Cheese Straws
Variety Crackers
Party Mix

Sweet
Papa's Sugar Cookies
Cherry Cordial Cookies
Whoopie Pies
Cream Wafers
Cranberry Braid
Granny's Fruit Cakes
Orange Juice Balls

Libations
Eggnog (non-alcoholic)
Christmas Tea
Variety Soft Drinks

Ham Delights

Norma Young

Never met anyone who didn't love these delightful treats!

2 trays Pepperidge Farms Party Rolls (or any tiny rolls - the kind that come in a foil tray in a sheet and each roll is about 1 by 2 inches)
1/2 - 1 pound boiled ham, shredded (dice with knife, or blend for second in processor)
1/3 pound Swiss cheese, sliced or grated

Spread:
1/2 pound butter
3 Tablespoons poppy seeds
1 teaspoon Worcestershire sauce
3 Tablespoons mustard
1 small to medium onion, chopped

Blend together spread. Split rolls in one piece horizontally, so that you have a sheet of roll tops and a sheet of roll bottoms. Spread on both sides.

Place bottom in tray, add meat, then cheese, then the tops of the rolls. Wrap in foil. Bake 10 minutes at 400 degrees or until hot through. Slice rolls apart. They freeze well and reheat well. Can be served hot or cold, on silver dish at a reception or in the foil tray while on a picnic or tailgating. Wonderful for traveling or as hors d'oeuvres.

Pigs in Blankets

A fun treat for the children that even a child can make with a table knife or plastic knife.

Hotdogs, or smoked sausages (these are fatter, you'll need more dough)

Crescent roll dough, from the refrigerator case (we call this "whop crescent rolls" from the sound the tube makes when you "whop" it on the counter)

Slice hotdogs in thirds across, to make short hotdogs.

"Whop" tube of crescent roll dough on the counter and carefully remove packaging. Roll dough out on clean surface, not separating the crescents. Gently mash perforations in the dough together to make one big sheet. Cut in strips about 3-4 inches by 1-2 inches.

Wrap a strip of dough around the middle of a hotdog piece and press to seal.

Bake at 350 degrees until dough is lightly browned.

Serve with ketchup and mustard or barbecue sauce.

Meat, Cheese & Other Trays

There's no need to spend a lot of money buying meat and cheese trays from the store, when all you need is a little creativity to make even nicer ones yourself.

Buy a variety of luncheon meats and cheeses, such as turkey, pastrami, roast beef and chicken for meats and cheddar, pepper jack, swiss, muenster, provolone and havarti for cheeses. We try to have sourdough, pumpernickel, rye and wheat breads, as well. Slice everything into a size appropriate for party sandwiches. For vegetables, we use broccoli, carrots, bell peppers, and grape tomatoes.

Choose a pretty plate or platter and arrange them in a pattern. Meat is very pretty rolled. Notice how the bread is sliced in half, or fourths, or if homemade, formed into tiny loaves. No one wants a whole sandwich when there is so much to sample. If the center is messy, you can add a piece of fruit, a flower or greenery for decoration – just use something edible or harmless.

Place mustard and mayonnaise in pretty bowls, goblets, or dessert dishes, as I did here, for a lovely presentation.

Savory Cheese Ball

8 oz cream cheese, very soft
8 oz extra sharp cheese, grated and room temperature
2 teaspoons Worcestershire sauce
1/8 teaspoon minced garlic, or pinch garlic powder
Splash hot sauce

Blend ingredients by hand. Form into a ball. Roll in pecan or walnut bits. Serve with crackers.

This is a very adaptable recipe. Feel free to adapt to your own taste.

Harral Young's Sugar Cookies

Everyone who has ever tried these say they are the best sugar cookies they've ever had!

3 ¼ cups all purpose flour
1 ½ cups sugar
2 eggs
2 ½ teaspoons baking powder
2 Tablespoons milk
2 teaspoons vanilla
½ teaspoon salt
2/3 cup real butter or shortening
½ teaspoon almond extract (mandatory, do not leave this out!)
Colored sugar (you can make your own with food coloring and sugar)

Cream butter, sugar, and eggs. Add other ingredients, beat until smooth. This is a stiff dough! Shape into a ball, wrap, and refrigerate at least 2-3 hours. Roll dough ¼ inch thick. Cut with cookie cutters. Dust with sugar or dip top into sugar. Place cookies ½ inch apart on greased cookie sheet. Bake at 400 degrees for 8 minutes.

The next two recipes come from my dear college friend Carolyn in Amish country. Carolyn is one of the best cookie bakers I know!

Whoopie Pies
Carolyn Shirley Tice

This are kind of like homemade "Little Debbies." They call them "gobs" too, in Amish country, but we prefer whoopie pies!

Cookies:
1/2 cup sugar
1/2 cup butter or shortening
2 eggs
1 cup milk
1 cup boiling water
1 teaspoon vanilla
4 cups flour
1 teaspoon baking soda
1 1/2 teaspoon salt
1/2 teaspoon baking powder
3/4 cup cocoa

Filling:
4 Tablespoons flour
3 Tablespoons butter (no substitutions)
1 cup milk
1/2 cup shortening (although I prefer butter in most things, shortening works better here - doesn't weep later)
3/4 cup sugar
1 teaspoon vanilla

Make cookie batter by creaming butter or shortening and sugar, then beating in the eggs. Add milk, boiling water, and vanilla, alternately with sifted dry ingredients. Mix well.

Drop by the tablespoonful on ungreased baking sheets and bake at 400 degrees for 5-7 minutes. Cool. (They will be soft, not crispy!)

For filling, make a white sauce by melting butter in skillet, stirring in flour until the flour begins to bubble well. (You just made a roux!) Stir in milk slowly. Cook until well-thickened, stirring constantly, then remove from heat and cool thoroughly. Add shortening, sugar and vanilla and beat until creamy.

Spread filling on flat bottom of a cookie. Press the flat bottom of another cookie to it to make a sandwich. Wrap in plastic wrap or cover tightly. These are big and filling!

CREAM WAFERS
Carolyn Shirley Tice

These are the most extraordinary little cookies. Absolutely irresistible!

Cookies:
1 cup soft real butter
1/3 cup whipping cream
2 cups flour

Filling: (Double for generous filling)
1/4 cup soft real butter
3/4 cup powdered sugar
1 teaspoon vanilla
Food coloring to tint

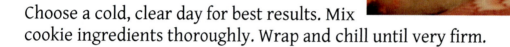

Choose a cold, clear day for best results. Mix cookie ingredients thoroughly. Wrap and chill until very firm.

Roll a third of less of dough at a time, keeping the rest refrigerated! Roll 1/8 inch thick on floured board (you can chill your board if dough is sticking). You may need to chill the rolled dough before cutting - you can stick it in the freezer for a couple of minutes to make it more easily handled.

Cut into 1½-inch rounds. Transfer rounds to plate of sugar and turn so both sides are coated. Place on ungreased cookie sheet and prick each round 3-4 times with fork. Bake for 7-9 minutes at 350 degrees. Cool.

Cream together filling. Tint to suit the occasion. Sandwich two wafers together with filling in the middle. We use red and green at Christmas, blue and pink for baby showers, bride's colors for bridal shower or wedding reception. Makes 7 - 7 1/2 dozen very tiny cookies.

Orange Juice Balls
Brenda Smith

An old-fashioned southern treat that seems to get better every year! This is a great recipe for your little ones to help with: lots of banging and goo, no eggs or baking.

1 pound crushed vanilla wafers (this is about 1¼ boxes or more now – boxes used to be a full pound!)
1 pound powdered sugar
1 stick butter, soft
1 6-ounce can orange juice concentrate, melted, but not reconstituted
Flaked coconut, less than a bag

Mix butter, sugar, melted orange juice concentrate and vanilla wafer crumbs. Form into small balls about 1 - 1 1/2 inches in diameter, or about a heaping teaspoonful. Roll in coconut while warm from your hands. Makes about 5 dozen balls.

Don't turn the page! Everything you've heard about fruit cake is not true of this one!

Granny's Fruit Cake
Lynwood Young

Like a rich lemon pound cake... with bonuses!

1 pound butter
1 pound brown sugar
6 eggs, separated
1/2 pound each: red and green candied cherries, cut.
1/2 pound cut pineapple
1 teaspoon baking powder
4 cups plain flour
2 cups chopped pecans (We often leave these out and use an extra half pound of pineapple)
1 1/2 ounces lemon extract

Cut cherries and pineapple in half with knife. Mix together and coat with 2 cups of flour.

Cream butter and sugar. Add egg yolks and beat. Sift together baking powder and 2 cups of the flour. Alternate adding sifted ingredients with adding extract.

Mix fruit and nuts into batter.

Beat egg whites and fold into batter.

Grease and flour a 10 inch tube pan (or smaller pans as described below) with wax paper cut to fit the bottom. Let stand overnight (I refrigerate).

Bake at 250 degrees foe 3 ½ hours. I cook mine in a variety of loaf pans from tiny ones to standard size to use for gifts - people like getting this fruitcake! They take less time to cook, too. Cook until a toothpick or straw comes out clean. It's forgiving, time-wise.

Cheese Straws
Young Family

Another great recipe to make with little ones – no eggs or raw stuff, lots of smushing! We have the young ones make these while the older ones make sausage balls.

½ pound extra sharp cheese
½ pound butter
¾ teaspoon salt
¼ teaspoon red pepper
2 cups plain flour
2 cups Rice Krispies

Blend grated cheese and soft butter. Add other ingredients in order. Drop from spoon in bite size pieces of stiff dough. Bake 18 minutes at 325 degrees. These can be made ahead, they keep very well and don't spread much during cooking.

Sausage Balls
Sluder Family Recipe

1 pound ground hot sausage, raw
3 cups biscuit mix (use Bisquick or see recipe below)
Worcestershire sauce, splash
1/2 pound sharp cheese

Dry Biscuit Mix:
2 1/2 cups plain flour
3/4 teaspoon salt
4 1/2 teaspoons baking powder
6 Tablespoons butter or shortening

Mix dry ingredients. Cut in butter. Mix all of the ingredients in a large bowl. Roll into 1 - 1 1/2 inch balls and place on a cookie sheet. Bake 15 minutes at 350 degrees. Serve hot or cold. Freezes well. *A favorite of the men in our family!*

Cordial Cookies

1 1/2 cups all-purpose flour
1/2 cup unsweetened cocoa powder
1/2 cup butter, softened
1 cup sugar
1/4 teaspoon baking soda
1/4 teaspoon baking powder
1 egg
1 1/2 teaspoons vanilla
48 maraschino cherries (about a jar), undrained.
1 cup semisweet chocolate chips
1/2 cup sweetened condensed milk

Preheat oven to 350. Cream butter and sugar. Beat in egg and vanilla. Add remaining dry ingredients. Dough will be stiff and pretty dry. Scoop a teaspoonful and roll into a ball. Place on cookie sheet an inch or two apart. Use your thumb to press a dent into center of cookie. Press a cherry into each dent. Heat milk and chips on low on stove, stirring to prevent burning. Add a tablespoon or two of cherry juice. Drip hot frosting on top until cherry is completely covered (important). Add more juice as necessary to keep pourable. Bake for ten minutes or so. Makes about 48 cookies.

Cranberry Braids

A lovely, Christmas-y treat.

Cranberry Sauce
1 12oz package cranberries
1 cup sugar
1 Tbs. cornstarch
1/3 cup orange juice

Braid dough
1 1/3 cup water
1 1/2 sticks butter
7 – 7 1/2 cups flour

4 1/2 teaspoons yeast

2/3 cup sugar

2 tablespoons grated orange rind

1 tsp. salt

4 eggs, one separated

Heat cranberry sauce ingredients on medium heat until cranberries break down and sauce thickens. Set aside or refrigerate to cool.

Melt butter and combine with warm water. Water should be quite hot to the touch, but not burn you. Add yeast.

Combine yeast, butter, and water with sugar. Separate one egg and save the egg white. Combine yolk with other eggs and beat. Combine eggs with yeast mixture. Add salt and orange rind. Slowly add flour while beating, then kneading until you have a smooth and elastic bread dough.

Place in a covered oiled bowl for an hour or two until the dent remains when you poke it. Divide dough into eight balls.

Take one ball of dough and roll it out into a rectangle. Ours usually end up about seven inches by 10 inches. Using a sharp knife or pizza cutter. Cut strips about one third of the way in on both sides every half inch or so, like below. The number of strips is not important, you just need the same number on both sides.

Brush center with egg white. Spread the cranberry sauce down the middle of the dough, staying about a half inch from either end and off of the strips. Starting at the top, pick up a strip from one side and pull it slightly diagonally over the cranberry sauce and press down just on the other side of it. Then do the same to a strip of dough on the other side. Continue, alternating sides, until you reach the bottom. Press the last strip down on the bottom edge, too.

Carefully lift the braid to a greased cookie sheet. Allow to sit in a warm place for about half an hour. Bake at 350 for 15 or 20 minutes, then brush with egg whites. Continue baking until done (when bread sounds hollow when you thump it). Let cool, then wrap tightly with plastic wrap for a lovely treat or gift.

What about Santa Claus?

We decided before we had children that we would be unable to continue the Santa Claus traditions of our youth. We both had pleasant memories of our parents pretending that Santa was real, but there were several things that made us uneasy. Santa Claus is portrayed as able to do anything (omnipotent), as being outside of time (able to go to every child's home during one night - omnipresent), and "knowing who's been bad or good" (omniscient). This is way too close to the attributes of God for us to tell our children about him, let them see seemingly physical proof of his existence (presents), then have them find out it was all pretend.

At the same time, we tell them about another wonderful Person who can do anything, be anywhere regardless of time or space, and knowing perfectly well who is bad or good. Oh, but this is different – God is *real*, and Santa is just *pretend*. Get it, kids?

Ouch.

We realized that what we were committed and duty-bound to teach our children about their Creator and Savior was critically important. Whether our children could trust us to speak the truth to them *always* could have an effect on whether they'd believe our story about God or have to hear it from someone who hadn't confused them with made-up stories so close to the real thing. If we decided that as much as it was up to us, we'd never tell our children a deliberate fiction, dressed up to be "truth" for a while, then that put the Santa tradition on the wrong side of the fence.

Did that take the joy out of Christmas for our children? By no means! We all have a joyous and exciting time and our boys are just as excited as any child to find out what is in their stockings and under the tree - even though, or perhaps especially because, they know their parents and siblings and grandparents put them there!

Does it make them into social pariahs? No, if we teach our children courtesy at the same time we explain the Santa Claus legend to them. We are very careful to tell them how important the Santa Claus story is to most families, and warn them it's not their place to debate child-rearing with adults. "What did Santa bring you?" should be answered with, "I'm so thankful I was given…" A knowledge of truth should never puff us up, and it's up to us as parents to coach our children on how to behave with humility and love toward others – especially well-meaning neighbors!

Christmas Gifts

We do not encourage rampant materialism in our home. For one thing, we can't afford it! We seldom watch TV, generally only at a relatives' house, so our children are not as inundated with advertising as most.

We've encouraged them to value the things we do: good, old books, family gifts we can all enjoy, family keepsakes and toys handed down from brothers or parents. They are normal children! They still enjoy getting toys and special gifts, but we try to be a little more creative than the latest "hot toy" everyone has got to have.

A lot of our well-meaning and very serious friends decry the commercialization of Christmas and avoid gift-giving at all – not wanting to encourage greed. The sin of greed is definitely something to avoid! And that's one reason we don't encourage our children to study catalogs or make lists like we did when we were younger. Nor do we seek out the hottest new toy or must have item for our children. We want them to greet whatever they are given with joy and thankfulness – and it's amazing how often the Lord gives them the desires of their hearts, too.

We do give gifts, though, and encourage gift-giving. After all, it is the Lord that gives good gifts to men and it is natural that we would desire to give gifts to those we love, too. There is a great joy in studying someone else's needs and desires and striving to meet them. In fact, that's what love is about, isn't it? Putting the needs and desires of others ahead of our own is what love really is. In that light, we think it's great to commemorate the greatest gift of all by gift giving.

We've seen our friends keep it under control a variety of ways. One family exchanges gifts on Old Christmas, Epiphany, January 6th, the day the wise men are commemorated. That makes sense, allows them to shop the after Christmas sales, and allows the parents to focus on more spiritual things at Christmas, making a break with the extreme excesses of their youth.

Another family gives one toy, one book, one piece of clothing to each child. Another draws names among the family and each person gives one big gift to their chosen recipient. They draw names at the *beginning* of the year, so they can think and plan for it all year.

Still another family always gives three gifts per person, like the three gifts mentioned that the wise men gave.

We haven't had much trouble with too many gifts since with all the health issues we've had in recent years, we have not had much extra to spend at all! A lot of folks are in that position this year, so how can we give good gifts to our children without spending a fortune?

One great money saving idea is to buy all year long as you see things go on sale or see them on craigslist or a yard sale. Many times children would rather have just what they want slightly used than something new they don't care for. We always check out the mark down aisles at the big box retailers, too. It's amazing how often the really great, classic toys get marked down to nothing. One year we were able to buy each of our boys model rockets for pennies on the dollar that way. We always put presents for the future under our bed and no one every looks there - our rule is that if you find it, you don't get it. We've never had to actually enforce that one!

Give useful things in a fun, festive way. Books they'll love, and you need for school next year, are great double-duty gifts. Clothes can be welcome if they are something they really want. We don't recommend the red briefs an elderly relative gave someone we know when he was young! Tools for a young man, or cooking implements for girls can sometimes be gotten very cheaply around Christmas. A young boy might be very happy with a new tool box with tools passed down from dad and grandpa.

You can also get out the sewing machine and make them costumes out of remnants, or sheets or tablecloths; or make a dolly sling or apron or tool apron. Hal's mother often gives family heirlooms or memorabilia as gifts. How grateful we were to be given Hal's ancestors' farm journal – what a treasure. And one year my uncle sent me photos of my father as a boy growing up. My father's been with the Lord for over 30 years and I'd rather have that than a diamond ring!

For our parents, ever since our first child was born, we have made a photo album or scrapbook of our year. We share photos from everything we do during the year and label them so they can refer to it for years. I am thinking we usually choose about 120 photos. We make three copies and three albums: one for Hal's folks, one for Melanie's and one for us - it would be awful to do all that and have nothing to enjoy in our own old age! We carefully watch for sales on photo-printing and on albums and we have been able to do this very cheaply. They aren't great examples of art, but they are treasured by the grandparents! In later

years, we've taken to doing a smaller album for the remaining great-grandparents and for our family that lives out of the country. I think these are the most popular gifts we give.

We use our baking for gifts for extended family and friends. We always try to send Hal's sister a big tray with at least one of everything we bake for everyone in her family. Her family is a lot smaller than ours and it just wouldn't make sense for her to bake as much as we do - they'd still be eating it in

July! - so I think our variety is a blessing to them. Likewise, we give our friends Fruitcake (Now, don't groan! Our fruitcake is most unusual and even more delicious!) or Cranberry Braid. Those homemade gifts not only show our love in a personal way, but they bless them with treats during the holidays.

One thing we've found out in our family is that the very best presents, the most memorable ones, are NOT the popular ones we spent a lot of money on. The best gifts are those given with a deep knowledge of the recipient, lots of love from the giver and a bunch of meaning in the gift.

And some years, the Lord just steps in. One year, we had no extra money except a small legacy from my grandmother. We didn't feel comfortable spending that on things soon forgotten. Then just a few weeks before Christmas, a music store in our area went out of business! We bought six or seven instruments for our family for the cost of half of one of them. Just perfect and we know my grandmother would have been delighted!

And then there's the year we found out Hal had cancer, while we had three children having surgery. I was completely unable to shop, with no time, if we did have money! I was so worried about it one night, I came home in tears, only to find an email from distant acquaintances saying, "Perhaps you'll think we're crazy, but we believe the Lord is leading us to buy your children Christmas presents!" Wow. His love for us extends even to this. It was one of the most wonderful Christmases we've ever had!

So, don't let gifts rule your season, let your gifts reflect your heart and soul!

Christmas Day

Our children are allowed to come downstairs and get their stockings whenever they wake on Christmas Day. They are full of candy, fruit and small gifts placed there at bedtime by different members of the family. It has amazed me to see how much our children love doing things like this for each other. One will buy a bag of special candy and keep it under his bed until he divides it into the stockings on Christmas Eve.

Our stockings are beautiful. They are each done in needlepoint by Hal's mother. Each time a new child is born, they use the one tiny stocking without a name that Granny made and by their second Christmas, she has a personalized one ready for them. I've seen some similar ones at Lands End for those of us who don't have the time or ability to make them.

When we get up, we usually have a special "quick and easy" breakfast. The past several years we've enjoyed Sausage Muffins. They freeze or refrigerate well, heat up quickly and can be carried around the house safely! The children are always anxious to open presents.

We gather in the living room with the tree and Hal explains to the children why we give gifts. We are remembering the greatest gift of all - Jesus Christ - who came to die on the cross in payment for our sins so that we could be forgiven and live forever with God. Then we take turns opening presents. Some families we know just all open presents at once, but we believe that the giver should be able to enjoy seeing the recipient's delight in his gift. Gifts aren't about material things, but are about relationships! What about when someone runs out of presents? Then they will be the designated opener for gifts for the family! We don't allow children to take presents out of their packages at this time, because we want each person to enjoy the opening and not be off to the side playing.

For Christmas dinner, we have a feast that doesn't require much attention during the morning; things Melanie can make ahead and just pop into the oven, since she wants to be with the family opening gifts and worshiping together.

So, at Thanksgiving, when we don't have a lot of obligations other than feasting, thankfulness, worship and teaching about what the Lord did through the Pilgrims, we pull out all stops on the cooking – making turkey and dressing, potatoes and gravy, homemade rolls, pies and lots more!

At Christmas on the other hand, we have ham and fixings. Melanie can get the ham in the pan the night before and just slide it in the oven. Similarly, we have mashed potatoes and gravy at Thanksgiving, but on Christmas we have a lovely old dish we called browned rice – it's rice cooked with onions and beef consomme´ -- so yum and requires just a minute or two to get it in the oven. We have escalloped pineapples, sweet potato soufflé and macaroni and cheese pie. All things Melanie can put together the day before and just bake on Christmas Day.

About 2 in the afternoon we have Christmas Dinner. The rest of the day, we spend singing carols (real Christmas hymns, not what passes for carols these days), playing together, playing games in the yard, visiting and going to church if services are being held.

"The Church does not superstitiously observe days, merely as days, but as memorials of important facts. Christmas might be kept as well upon one day of the year as another; but there should be a stated day for commemorating the birth of our Saviour, because there is danger that what may be done on any day, will be neglected."

Samuel Johnson

Sausage Muffins
Brenda Smith

A great, easy Christmas morning breakfast!

2lb bulk breakfast sausage
3 jars (5oz each) Kraft Old English cheese (or make your own cheese sauce)
18 English muffins

Brown sausage, drain. Add cheese while sausage is hot.

Split muffins, spread mixture on muffins. Freeze or refrigerate until ready to use.

Toast in oven or toaster oven until hot through. Yummy! To save money, I've made my own cheese sauce, too, by making a thick white sauce and adding grated sharp cheese. Or, you can use any Velveeta-type melting cheese, though a sharp one is best.

You may need to prepare this in secret to keep the batch from disappearing from "tasters."

Christmas Dinner Menu

Baked Ham
Escalloped Pineapple
Browned Rice
Seven Layer Salad
Macaroni and Cheese Pie
Sweet Potato Soufflé
Vegetables
Hot Rolls
Chocolate Pie
Blueberry or Apple Pie
Egg Custard Pie

BAKED HAM

A fully cooked smoked ham, whole or butt portion
Pineapple slices
Cloves
Brown sugar
Cranberries, Pomegranate, or Maraschino Cherries, optional
Toothpicks, if using cranberries or cherries.

Place the ham cut side down, if any. Score the skin diagonally in two directions to make diamond shape marks.

Pour a cup of so of water in the bottom of the roaster and cover the ham with foil.

Bake at 350 for 15-20 minutes per pound for a whole ham or 20-25 minutes per pound for a half, or until internal temperature is 160 degrees, or as marked on the package.

About a half hour before the ham is done, remove from the oven, sprinkle brown sugar all over the top and use cloves to stick pineapple slices to the skin of the ham in a pretty pattern. Use toothpicks to stick cranberries or cherries in the pineapple centers, if desired.

Escalloped Pineapple
Aunt Lucy Godshall

Just the absolute best side dish for ham ever. Exquisite.

4 beaten eggs
1 stick butter (1/2 cup), melted
1 cup sugar
5 slices bread cubed (use enough to make 1 quart of bread cubes, may take more slices than this)
1 can (15-20 oz) crushed pineapple, with the juice

Mix melted butter, sugar and eggs. Stir in pineapple with its juice. Stir in bread crumbs. Refrigerate until ready to bake (overnight is fine, so is cooking immediately). Bake at 300 degrees for 45 minutes to 1 hour, or until edges are crispy and center is firm. Serve with ham. Everyone we've ever served this to begs for the recipe. Honestly, we don't serve ham without it. Ever.

Browned Rice
Brenda Smith

½ stick real butter
One onion, diced
2 cups rice
2 - 10 ½ oz cans beef consommé (find in soup section near beef broth)
1 can water

Melt butter and sauté onions and rice until onions are transparent and rice is browning.

Transfer mixture to casserole dish. Choose one with a lid or cover with foil. Pour consommé and water over the rice.

Bake at 350 degrees until all liquid is mostly absorbed and rice is tender.

Seven Layer Salad

When you need to make a salad in advance, this classic can't be beat!

½ -1 pound of bacon, cooked, drained and crumbled
1 large head of sturdy lettuce, such as Iceberg or Romaine
1 sweet onion or a bunch of green onions, chopped
1 10-ounce package of frozen green peas
½ pound to one pound cheddar cheese, grated, sharp tastes best to me
1 large bell pepper, chopped
3-6 hard-boiled eggs, sliced or chopped (optional, but delicious)
1 cup of mayonnaise or Miracle Whip type salad dressing
2 Tablespoons sugar or brown sugar

Tear lettuce into bite size pieces. Put about half in a glass casserole dish (we usually use a 9x13 inch); Glass so you can see the pretty layers!

Starting with the lettuce, layer a third of the onions, peas, peppers, cheese and egg (if used) one at a time. Repeat until finished.

Spread the salad dressing type mayonnaise across top, being very careful to spread all the way to the edges and cover the entire casserole to keep it fresh in the fridge. Sprinkle the brown sugar, then the bacon on top. Good variations include grated carrots, finely chopped cauliflower or broccoli, craisins or raisins. Cover and chill overnight. You won't believe how delicious and fresh this is!

Nanny's Macaroni and Cheese Pie

Melanie's grandmother had the most wonderful cook, Nanny, who made this macaroni and cheese at every holiday meal. We children were sent into the kitchen to spy out the recipe since Nanny didn't allow adults in her kitchen and didn't share recipes.
It is still that good!
Hal's grandmother was also known for her macaroni and cheese; this is just like hers.

1 pound macaroni noodles (small elbow macaroni)
1 1/2 pounds extra sharp cheddar cheese (the sharper, the better), grated
4 eggs, beaten
4 cups milk
1 teaspoon salt
1/4 teaspoon pepper
butter, to dot

Boil macaroni ten minutes, drain. Layer cheese with macaroni in a casserole dish. You really can't use too much cheese. The more you use, the better it will be. End with cheese on top, completely covering the macaroni. Stop here to refrigerate overnight if you want to make ahead.

Mix remaining ingredients together and pour over. Dot with butter and sprinkle with pepper.

Bake at 350 degrees for 45 minutes or until set.

Sweet Potato Souffle

About 5-6 large sweet potatoes (large is a relative term, you want about 5 cups mashed)
½ stick butter (1/4 cup)
¾-1 cup brown sugar (taste and add more if you like it sweeter)
3 eggs
1 teaspoon vanilla
½ cup orange juice, cream, evaporated milk or milk
½ teaspoon salt
1 teaspoon cinnamon
½ teaspoon nutmeg
½ cup raisins, regular or golden
Bag large marshmallows

Peel and boil sweet potatoes until soft. Drain and Immediately add butter. Add liquid and mash with beaters. Add eggs and seasonings. Stir in raisins. Spread in a casserole dish. Stop at this point if you'd like to prepare ahead and refrigerate.

Heat at 350 degrees until piping hot. Takes about 30-45 minutes, depending on starting temperature. Remove from the oven and put marshmallows on top. Return to oven (on broil if you need them quickly) and cook until marshmallows begin to brown on top. Keep an eye on them! Serve hot.

Chocolate Meringue Pie

2 large 5 oz boxes Jello Cook and Serve Pudding and Pie Filling, Chocolate
6 cups whole milk
2 single pie crusts, If I buy them, I prefer the rolled kind found in the refrigerated section of the store
4 eggs, separated, at room temperature, with no yolk in the whites at all
Pinch of cream of tartar, optional, but helps
6 Tablespoons sugar
1 teaspoon vanilla extract
2 pie pans, glass is prettiest

This is a simple recipe using many bought ingredients, but it is just exactly the one I grew to love growing up. I can make it from scratch now, but why not do something easy when you are already so busy?

Cook the pudding mix in a saucepan according to the directions.

While it is heating, roll out the dough and lift into the pans. Trim the edges at the edge of the pan. An easy pretty edge can be made by putting your two index fingers just a thumbwidth apart on the edge, then using your thumb between them to poke the edge up there slightly to one side. Continue around to make a pretty scalloped edge.

Prick the bottom and bake at 350 until just beginning to brown.

When the pudding is boiling briskly and thickening, beat the egg yolks and add just a small spoonful of pudding and stir it into the eggs. Add a little larger spoonful of pudding and stir in. This warms the eggs gradually and will keep them from scrambling as you put them in the pudding. Once it's about half and half eggs and pudding, add the eggs to the pudding and stir in. Take the pudding off the heat and stir a time or two and pour into the pie crusts. Set aside.

In a perfectly clean bowl and using completely clean mixer paddles, begin beating the egg whites. When frothy, add the cream of tartar. This stabilizes the egg whites and makes it easy to produce a nice meringue.

Beat until almost stiff, then slowly add the sugar, beating all the time.

Add vanilla while continuing to beat. Stop when the peaks stand up and just the end droops down.

Spread meringue over the hot pies, being very sure indeed to cover every inch of the filling and touch the pastry on every side. This helps keep the meringue from shrinking in the fridge.

Bake the pie at 350 degrees until the meringue begins to brown prettily on the peaks, but is still a lovely light brown. Refrigerate until serving. Makes two pies.

Egg Custard Pie

The directions in The Joy of Cooking by Irma Rombauer are incomparable.

Pumpkin Cheesecake Pie

The recipe for this wonderful pie is in our book, Christ-Centered Thanksgiving.

OLD CHRISTMAS

We really love history and we really love the holiday season. Put the two together and you get, "Old Christmas." Traditionally, the twelve days of Christmas were the days between Christmas, December 25th and Epiphany, January 6th. Just as Christmas is traditionally the day of Christ's birth, Epiphany is traditionally the day the wise men came and worshipped the Christ Child. In many places, that was the day that gifts were exchanged, just as the wise men brought gifts to honor the King of Kings.

We have put together a family tradition around Epiphany. January 6th is the end of the Christmas season for us. That's the day that we "un-decorate" the house and tree. We make a celebration out of this, too. Yes, Youngs do love to celebrate!

Adoration of the Magi, Peter Paul Rubens

This is the last time that we sing the Christmas carols and drink eggnog until next year's Advent. We read this part of the Christmas story to our children and talk about what it means. We love to have party foods one last time and finish off any that remain from our baking. Then we take down the tree and pack up all our treasures. We take our time with this and talk about the memories we've associated with each of our ornaments and decorations – the people that gave them to us, the years that have passed, the mercies of God that we have seen.

We are definitely the last family in the neighborhood to bring down the decorations, but it seems such a shame to take them down right after Christmas, when that week or so is generally a quiet and family-oriented time and we can enjoy them.

It's our hope and prayer that all of our traditions, both at Christmas and other times of the year will make markers in our children's memories; that as they smell cloves they will remember the happy times drinking Christmas tea at home and think about the things we taught them. That when they hear the Christmas carols on the radio, they'll think about the joy and laughter going caroling with friends and they will remember that Christians don't have to ape the world to have fun. The goal of all of these traditions is to tie our children's hearts to the Lord – to point to His majesty, His graciousness, His provision.

Thank you for allowing us to share our family traditions with you! We hope that we have given you ideas for your own family. We pray that you will develop family traditions that will glorify God and draw your children's hearts toward home, for, as Theodore Kuyler wrote, "Everything that attracts our children to their homes is very apt to be, in the end, an attraction towards heaven."

Merry Christmas!

When I think of Christmas Eves, Christmas feasts, Christmas songs, and Christmas stories, I know that they do not represent a short or transient gladness. Instead, they speak of a joy unspeakable and full of glory. God loved the world and sent His Son. Whosoever believes in Him will not perish, but have everlasting life. That is Christmas joy. That is the Christmas spirit."

Corrie ten Boom

Our Other Resources

Find our other resources, including great character-building gifts, at our site: www.RaisingRealMen.com.

Join our online community

RaisingRealMen.com Our blog and store.

Facebook.com/raisingrealmen_Tens of thousands of people discussing raising godly sons!

Facebook.com/HalandMelanie

Twitter.com/raisingrealmen

Pinterest.com/raisingrealmen

Instagram.com/raisingrealmen

And If You Enjoyed This Book, Take a Look at Christ-Centered Thanksgiving

Acknowledgements

All of our work flows out of the good gifts of God the Father, who sent His Son, Jesus Christ to pay the penalty for our sin. All glory is His alone. Every day is Christmas for the redeemed.

We are grateful for our eight great children, who help us and bless us in so many ways. Thanks, guys!

We especially want to thank the many great cooks in our lives – Nana, Granny, Grand-Nana, Mama Helen, the original Granny, Grandma, Nanny, and all those who have influenced us in our celebration of Christmas, including our fathers, especially. That influence is evident in these pages. Thank you!

We are especially grateful to Norma Young, Hal's mother, for the use of her original painting for the cover of this work.

Images

Advent Wreath, Bubamara, Wikimedia Commons,
http://commons.wikimedia.org/wiki/File:Adventn%C3%BD_veniec_V.jpg
Old Dutch Bible 4, Taluda, Stock Exchange,
http://www.sxc.hu/browse.phtml?f=download&id=991901
Carolers, juliaf, Stock Exchange,
http://www.sxc.hu/browse.phtml?f=download&id=657688

All other images ©2006-2016 Hal & Melanie Young or John Calvin Young, All Rights Reserved

Made in the USA
Middletown, DE
03 December 2023